Celebrate the First Thanksgiving

with Elaine Landau

Enslow Elementary

an imprint of

 Enslow Publishers, Inc.

40 Industrial Road   PO Box 38
Box 398   Aldershot
Berkeley Heights, NJ 07922   Hants GU12 6BP
USA   UK

http://www.enslow.com

Enslow Elementary, an imprint of Enslow Publishers, Inc.

Enslow Elementary® is a registered trademark of Enslow Publishers, Inc.

Library of Congress Cataloging-in-Publication Data:

Landau, Elaine.
    Celebrate the first Thanksgiving with Elaine Landau / by Elaine Landau.
       p. cm. — (Explore Colonial America with Elaine Landau)
    Includes bibliographical references and index.
    ISBN 0-7660-2556-X
    1. Massachusetts—History—New Plymouth, 1620–1691—Juvenile literature. 2. Pilgrims (New Plymouth Colony)—Juvenile literature. 3. Wampanoag Indians—Juvenile literature. 4. Thanksgiving Day—Juvenile literature. I. Title. II. Series.
    F68.L23 2006
    974.4'02—dc22   2005018314

Printed in the United States of America

10 9 8 7 6 5 4 3 2 1

To Our Readers: We have done our best to make sure all Internet Addresses in this book were active and appropriate when we went to press. However, the author and the publisher have no control over and assume no liability for the material available on those Internet sites or on other Web sites they may link to. Any comments or suggestions can be sent by e-mail to comments@enslow.com or to the address on the back cover.

Series Literacy Consultant: Allan A. De Fina, Ph.D., Past President of the New Jersey Reading Association and Professor, Department of Literacy Education, New Jersey City University.

Contents

PLYMOUTH
COLONY
1620

KEY
 = American Indian Village
→ = Route of the *Mayflower*

This is what an early Pilgrim house looked like.

NORTH AMERICA

Plymouth

Atlantic Ocean

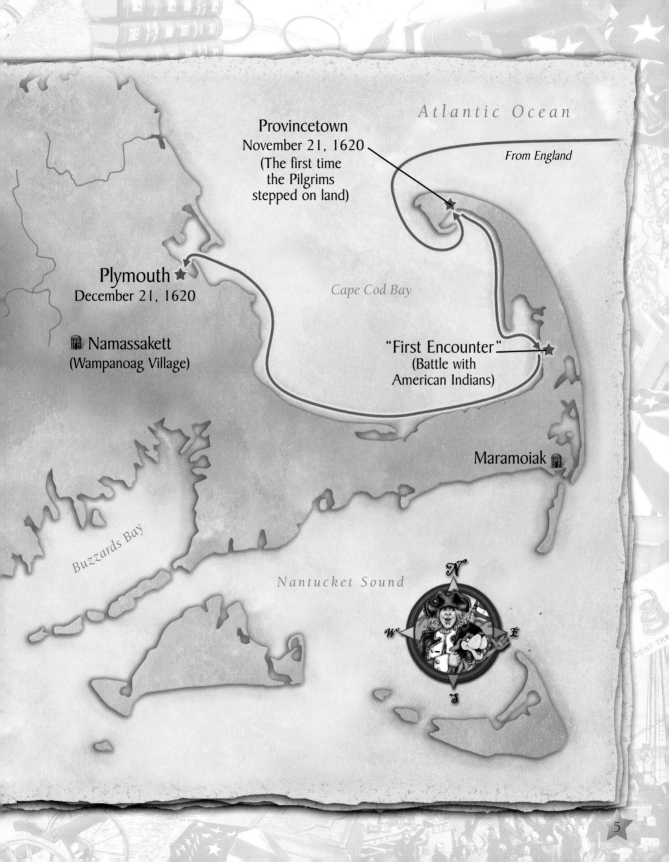

Atlantic Ocean

Provincetown
November 21, 1620
(The first time
the Pilgrims
stepped on land)

From England

Plymouth
December 21, 1620

Cape Cod Bay

Namassakett
(Wampanoag Village)

"First Encounter"
(Battle with
American Indians)

Maramoiak

Buzzards Bay

Nantucket Sound

N
W   E
S

5

Dear Fellow Explorer,

What if you had a time machine? Imagine turning a dial to step back into history. Where would you go? Would you want to see America the way it was long ago?

Would you bravely board the Mayflower with the Pilgrims? There would be lots of hard work. There would also be danger. But there would be adventure and excitement, too.

This hat was owned by the Pilgrim Constance Hopkins. The colonists made the hat from beaver skin.

A replica of the original *Mayflower* sails near Massachusetts.

6

The Pilgrims held the First Thanksgiving to thank God for the harvest they had received.

I am Elaine Landau and this is my dog, Max. Max and I do lots of time traveling. Now he wants to sail on the Mayflower. Max also wants to see what food was on the first Thanksgiving menu.

Why not come along with us? Use this book as your time machine. We will meet the Pilgrims and the Wampanoag Indians. Maybe they will invite us to dinner—Thanksgiving dinner, that is.

Are you ready for takeoff? Start thinking of a Wampanoag village. Now turn the page. Blast off!

HEY, DIDN'T THE PILGRIMS WEAR BLACK AND WHITE OUTFITS?

JUST ON SUNDAYS AND SPECIAL OCCASIONS. OTHER TIMES, THEY WORE COLORFUL CLOTHING.

The Wampanoag

Long before Europeans came to North America, other people lived there. These were American Indians. Among them was a group we know as the Wampanoag. They mostly lived along the shores of Massachusetts and on nearby islands.

The Wampanoag were peaceful people who farmed, fished, and hunted. Family ties were strong among them. Both the old and the young were well cared for.

The Wampanoag had never seen a European until the 1500s. That was when explorers, fishermen, and traders began arriving. They did not stay in North America long. Yet, they left behind diseases from Europe.

Often, these diseases were deadly to American Indians. Their bodies were not used

The Wampanoag made canoes by carving tree trunks. Sometimes, they burned the inside of the log to hollow it out. This modern Wampanoag shows how to make a canoe.

8

THE WAMPANOAG WORKED REALLY HARD.

THEY WERE ALSO KNOWN FOR THEIR KINDNESS TO VISITORS. THEY OFTEN SHARED THEIR FOOD WITH THEM.

to them. Sometimes disease wiped out whole villages.

That happened to the Patuxet Indians. The Patuxet were close relatives of the Wampanoag and had lived nearby. Nearly every person in the Patuxet village died from a disease that may have been smallpox. The few who lived went to stay with the Wampanoag.

By the early 1600s, more Europeans came to North America. Now they brought their families. They also brought guns and ammunition. These Europeans had come to stay in America.

The settlers wanted the American Indians out of the way. They wanted to take their land. In time, the American Indians feared for both their land and their lives.

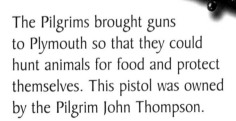

The Pilgrims brought guns to Plymouth so that they could hunt animals for food and protect themselves. This pistol was owned by the Pilgrim John Thompson.

9

2 Crossing the Atlantic

September 6, 1620. A 100-foot wooden ship named the *Mayflower* had just set sail from Plymouth, England. Inside, 102 passengers were starting an exciting journey. They were leaving England to start a new life in North America.

Crossing the Atlantic would take about two months. At first, the weather was mild. But those pleasant days gave way to powerful storms. Fierce winds and high waves tossed the vessel about on the ocean.

This replica of the *Mayflower* is docked near Plymouth, Massachusetts, today.

The *Mayflower* had a rough trip across the Atlantic Ocean.

The food aboard the *Mayflower* was very simple. Near the top are hard biscuits. At the bottom is a bowl of dried peas.

The stormy weather was very hard on the passengers. Many became extremely seasick. Some of them found it hard to stand. Some passengers remained below deck for most of the voyage. That area was usually used to carry cargo. Now it held people as well as the farm animals taken on the journey.

A large number of the Pilgrims could not even keep their food down. Not that there was much to eat anyway. The passengers had some salted pork, beef, and dried codfish. All the cheese had gone **moldy**. **Maggots** and rats had gotten into the hard biscuits and dried peas.

Some on board became quite ill. Before the trip was over, two people on the *Mayflower* died. One was a passenger and the other a sailor.

THESE STORMS ARE DANGEROUS. ONE OF THE PILGRIMS FELL OVERBOARD.

LUCKILY, HE CLUNG TO THE ROPES ON THE SHIP'S SIDES AND THE CREW PULLED HIM BACK UP.

Later on, strong winds caused a beam on the main deck to crack. If it were not repaired, the ship could develop a serious leak. This scared some of the passengers and seamen. Several wanted to turn back. However, it was soon fixed and the *Mayflower* stayed on course.

There were some joyful moments too. During the voyage, a woman named Elizabeth Hopkins gave birth. She and her husband, Stephen, gave their new son a fitting name. The boy was called Oceanus.

Some historians believe that this was the cradle of Oceanus Hopkins.

3 Land Ho!

Finally, two months after they had left, the Pilgrims spotted land on November 9, 1620. They had arrived at the tip of the area now known as Cape Cod. The passengers hugged one another and celebrated. Some dropped to their knees to give thanks.

The *Mayflower* passengers had not had enough money for their voyage. A group of businessmen had paid for it. However, the trip was not a gift. The settlers would have to pay them back. They were to do so with furs, fish, and lumber from North America.

No one knew if these Pilgrims could build a thriving colony. Some on board had their doubts. The *Mayflower* passengers did not always get along.

Forty-six of them had left England for religious reasons. These were known as Separatists. The Separatists had separated from the Church of England. They wanted to worship in their own way and felt unable to do this in England. Now they hoped to start a colony in North America where they could worship as they pleased.

The Pilgrims had to hunt animals to get furs. They needed the fur to pay back the money they had borrowed.

14

In both England and Plymouth Colony, the Saints would dress in black and white and go to a church service every Sunday.

The Separatists that came to New England called themselves Saints. Not all the *Mayflower* passengers were Saints. The Saints called the others on board Strangers. The Strangers were not coming to North America for religious reasons. They came to build a better life for themselves. Some hoped to become wealthy.

Today, we call both the Saints and the Strangers Pilgrims. However, a "pilgrim" is someone taking a religious journey. This was not true of all the *Mayflower* passengers.

The Saints did not quite trust the Strangers. The Strangers did not care for the Saints either. They did not like the Saints telling them how they should live their lives. Nevertheless, both groups would have to live together in North America.

Some things needed to be worked out. This was especially important because the storms had thrown the ship off course. The settlers had not planned to land this far north.

They had made an arrangement with the Virginia Company of London to start a colony in the area known as present-day New York State. The Virginia Company needed more settlers in North America. Its first colony in Jamestown, Virginia, was not doing well.

A halberd was a special type of weapon that the Pilgrims only used for ceremonies. Also, a person who owned one was considered very important. This one was owned by John Alden, who was once assistant governor of Plymouth Colony.

But the Virginia Company did not control the territory this far north. Settling on uncharted land worried some on the *Mayflower*. Would everyone still follow the terms of the original agreement?

To make sure they did, the *Mayflower* passengers drew up their own agreement. It would later be called the Mayflower Compact.

On November 11, 1620, both Saints and Strangers signed the Mayflower Compact.

The Mayflower Compact helped the Pilgrims choose their leaders before they even set foot on the strange new land.

Through it, they agreed to pass laws and elect officials. This helped start an important tradition in American government—the direct election of our leaders.

Before leaving the ship, a Saint named John Carver was elected governor of their colony. Carver was a successful businessman. He was also known to be fair.

Everyone felt better after signing an agreement. Yet no one could be sure how things would really turn out. Now they could only work hard and hope for the best.

IT'S NOT FAIR. NO WOMEN SIGNED THE COMPACT.

BACK THEN, WOMEN HAD NO LEGAL RIGHTS.

17

4 Finding a Place

Everyone on the *Mayflower* had been glad to reach land. Yet the passengers were still uneasy. They did not know if there were American Indians nearby.

So not everyone left the ship at once. On November 11, a group of sixteen men went ashore first. They later returned safely with firewood.

Two days later, all the passengers left the *Mayflower*. The children played on the beach while the women washed clothes. Some of the men went exploring.

The first group of men that left the *Mayflower* explored the land to make sure it was safe for the others.

They soon found some empty wigwams. These were round-roofed houses

The *Mayflower* could not go close to shore because the bottom of it could get damaged by scraping across the sea floor. In order to land on shore, the Pilgrims had to use a smaller boat that was carried over on the *Mayflower*.

that belonged to the Wampanoag Indians. The Pilgrims took whatever they pleased from these. They carried out food, tools, blankets, and baskets.

They also found the American Indians' supply of dried corn. The Wampanoag had buried it in the ground. The Pilgrims dug it up and took it with them. They did not see this as wrong. This was partly because they did not respect the Indians. They wrongly believed that American Indians were **savages**. They also thought that God had put these supplies in their path so they could take them.

The Wampanoag lived in round houses before the European settlers came.

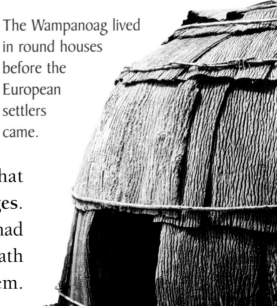

However, when they finally met the owners of the corn later, they paid them for what they took.

The *Mayflower* settlers did not remain at Cape Cod for long. It was not the best place to settle. There was no source of fresh water in sight. Some settlers also became ill after eating the **mussels** they found on the shore.

The Pilgrims had a smaller boat with them on the *Mayflower*. This vessel could sail safely in **shallow** waters. An exploring party of eighteen men was formed. They sailed out to see the broader area. Among those who went were Governor Carver, another Saint named William Bradford, and Captain Miles Standish, a military man. On December 8, 1620, these men spotted some American Indians and exchanged shots with them. The spot on Cape Cod where this took place came to be known as "the First Encounter."

William Bradford was the Pilgrims' governor for over thirty years. He also wrote a history of the colony called *Of Plimoth Plantation*.

The Pilgrims continued to look for a good place for the colony. Then on December 11, the men found the perfect spot. It was the area that we know today as Plymouth, Massachusetts. Plymouth

HEY, I THOUGHT THE PILGRIMS STEPPED ON PLYMOUTH ROCK WHEN THEY ARRIVED.

ACTUALLY, MAX, THERE'S NO RECORD THAT THEY REALLY DID!

was a good site for a new colony. The Pilgrims found fresh water there. There were cleared fields in which to

plant crops. Captain Miles Standish had wanted a place that they could easily defend. This site even had a hill where Standish could build a fort. The Pilgrims felt that they could make their new home there. It was a good choice.

Miles Standish was respected by the Pilgrims for his military and organizational skills.

5 *A Place Picked Twice*

The rest of the *Mayflower* passengers soon followed the exploring party. They arrived in Plymouth on December 16. The weather was growing colder and there had already been some heavy snows.

The new settlers needed to build shelters. There was no time to waste. They cut down some trees to quickly build shelters. The men also built a **palisade** or barrier of logs around the village. This was done for protection.

The new settlers had worried about Indian attacks. Even before leaving England, they had heard about attacks on the Jamestown colony. They had also briefly battled with the Indians during "the First Encounter" on Cape Cod. However, so far, no American Indians had come to their settlement.

Both Saints and Strangers had to work together to build houses before the harsh winter came.

Miles Standish built a fort on top of a hill. From there, he could see the surrounding woods, the settlement of Plymouth, and any approaching ships in the ocean.

Yet, the Pilgrims never felt safe. There were wolves in the surrounding woods. Sometimes they could be heard howling at night.

In the distance, the Pilgrims also often saw smoke. It came from American Indian campfires. Now and then a settler would see an American Indian in the woods. The Pilgrims did not know what to expect.

Later, they learned more about their Wampanoag neighbors. The spot the Pilgrims picked for their colony was well known to these American Indians. It was once a Patuxet Indian village.

That was the reason why the Pilgrims had found cleared fields there. The Patuxet Indians had used these to plant corn. Now the Pilgrims would try to plant their crops there.

MILES STANDISH PLACED THEIR LARGEST CANNON ON FORT HILL.

HE WAS ALSO GIVEN THE HOUSE CLOSEST TO THE HILL SO HE COULD ACT QUICKLY IF THEY WERE ATTACKED.

23

6 The General Sickness

The Pilgrims' first winter at Plymouth was hard. Many of these new settlers were weak and tired. The long voyage from England had taken its toll. Before long, some settlers became very ill.

A number of them developed a disease called scurvy. This comes from not getting enough Vitamin C. This vitamin is commonly found in fresh fruits and vegetables. Such foods were scarce on the voyage.

The Pilgrims with scurvy suffered. Their gums bled and their teeth fell out. Their joints ached and they always felt weak.

A Pilgrim with the "General Sickness" spent a lot of time in bed.

Some of the settlers probably also had typhus, another deadly disease. These Pilgrims ran high fevers. They had headaches and chills. Some had a rash that covered much of their body. The Pilgrims called their illnesses "the General Sickness."

They tried to nurse their loved ones back to health. But many people grew weaker each day. As the weeks passed, large numbers of them died. There was little time to mourn. They had to bury their dead to prevent more disease.

This was often done at night. The Pilgrims knew that the American Indians were watching them. They were still afraid of being attacked. They did not want the Indians to know how few settlers were left.

Meanwhile, the Pilgrims still needed to learn a great deal. They had no idea where the best fishing spots were. They were not very skilled at tracking animals either. They also did not know what crops would grow best in the area's rocky soil.

As a result, there was little food. The Pilgrims tried to get by on what they could find. They lived on nuts from trees, and clams and mussels from the ocean but there was never enough. Everyone was always hungry. As they grew weaker, it became harder for them to work.

By March 31, 1621, nearly half the settlers who came over on the *Mayflower* had died of sickness or starvation. The ship had not returned to England yet. Many of its crew had died as well. Almost every family had lost someone. People wondered how they could go on. Yet they found the courage to do so.

THIS FELLOW SEEMS TO BE DOING BETTER.

I JUST WISH THAT WE COULD DO MORE TO HELP.

Clams and mussels helped the Pilgrims survive.

25

7 The Arrival of Samoset

During the winter, the American Indians had stayed away from the colony. However, the Pilgrims knew that they were nearby. On February 16, 1621, a settler saw about a dozen American Indians in the forest. He quickly ran back to the colony. He told the others that the American Indians might be on their way there.

After surviving a hard winter, the Pilgrims had very little to bake in their ovens.

The Pilgrims prepared for an attack. They brought a cannon from the *Mayflower* to the colony. Captain Standish formed a tiny fighting force of settlers.

The Pilgrims were prepared for the worst. But none of the American Indians the settler saw ever came. Then on March 16, 1621, one American Indian walked into the colony. His name was Samoset.

Samoset was friendly toward the Pilgrims.

Samoset appeared at the doorway of the Pilgrims' meetinghouse. The Pilgrims were shocked to see him standing there. They were even more surprised to hear him speak English.

Samoset had learned English from English fishermen. He had sailed with them along the Atlantic coast. Samoset told the Pilgrims about their neighbors—the Wampanoag Indians. He explained how they had lived in this area for many years. Samoset also spoke about a great

Massasoit was the great chief of the Wampanoag.

YES, IT'S A GOOD THING THAT THE WAMPANOAG WERE PEACEFUL TOWARD THE PILGRIMS.

TRADING WITH THE WAMPANOAG REALLY HELPED THE PILGRIMS.

Wampanoag chief named Massasoit.

Since it was getting late, Samoset spent the night with the Pilgrims. He stayed in the home of Elizabeth and Stephen Hopkins. The Hopkinses tried to make Samoset comfortable. He left the next morning in a very good mood.

The next day, Samoset returned to the colony. This time, he came with five other Wampanoag Indians. They brought beaver **pelts** (skins) for the settlers.

The Pilgrims were delighted with the pelts. They hoped the Wampanoag would begin trading with them. The settlers had brought trinkets and shiny knives to trade with the American Indians. The Pilgrims became hopeful. It looked like the Wampanoag would not be their enemy. Instead, they would help the colony survive.

The Pilgrims were able to use beaver furs to make warm clothes for the winter. They could also trade beaver furs to the Wampanoag or England.

8 Squanto

On March 22, Samoset came back to the colony. That day he brought an American Indian named Tisquantum with him. This new visitor also spoke English. The English gave Tisquantum the nickname "Squanto."

Years ago, Squanto had been captured by an English sea captain. The captain took him to Europe. There Squanto was sold into slavery. He was somehow able to escape and return home on an English fishing ship.

However, he had a painful homecoming. Squanto was a Patuxet Indian. He returned to a village wiped out by disease. So he went to live with the Wampanoag.

Now Squanto decided to help the Pilgrims. He stayed at the colony. He taught the Pilgrims everything they needed to know.

Squanto taught the Pilgrims new ways to fish. Squanto could catch eels with his feet. Before long, the Pilgrims were digging for clams. They set traps for lobsters too. Having enough meat was

Squanto taught the Pilgrims how to set traps for lobsters.

Squanto helped the Pilgrims learn how to live off the land.

Squash and beans became important foods for the Pilgrims after Squanto taught the settlers how to grow them.

important to the Pilgrims. So Squanto taught the men how to track and hunt animals.

By spring, it was time to plant crops. Squanto brought the Pilgrims seeds to grow corn, peas, squash, and beans. Squanto also showed the settlers which nuts, fruits, and berries were safe to eat. He even taught them how to use plants and herbs as medicines.

Through Squanto, the Pilgrims met Massasoit, a great Wampanoag chief. On March 23, 1621, Massasoit and the Pilgrims signed a peace **treaty**. The peace between them would last over fifty years.

On April 5, 1621, the *Mayflower* set sail for England. None of the colonists chose to leave

SQUANTO TOLD THE PILGRIMS TO PUT A DEAD FISH IN THE SOIL WITH THEIR SEEDS.

THE FISH IS A TYPE OF FERTILIZER, WHICH HELPS PLANTS GROW.

32

When Massasoit came to sign the peace treaty, he brought a group of Wampanoag warriors with him.

with the ship. With Squanto's help, they were there to stay. However, they still had a lot of hard work to do over the summer. They had to do all they could to make sure they had plenty of food for the winter.

The American Indians' main crop was corn. Sometimes they dried it and ground it into a powder called corn meal. They would then use the corn meal to make bread.

9 A Harvest Celebration

The spring and summer of 1621 went well for the Pilgrims. By fall, they had had a good corn harvest. Fish and game had been plentiful too. It looked like the colony would survive another winter.

The colony's new governor was William Bradford. Bradford was pleased with things. He decided to have a feast to celebrate.

The Pilgrims were grateful for Squanto's help. They invited him to the feast. They also invited the Wampanoag Indian chief Massasoit.

The day of the feast, Massasoit, along with ninety Wampanoag men, arrived at the colony. They brought food to share with everyone there. The Wampanoag even brought five deer to eat.

With Squanto's help, the Pilgrims soon had plenty of food on the table. (These Pilgrims are being played by modern people.)

Great feasting took place at the first Thanksgiving.

No one knows the exact date of the feast. But it was probably in the middle of October. No one knows exactly what was served at this celebration either.

However, Governor Bradford had sent four men out to hunt for the feast. It is likely that they brought back wild turkeys, geese, ducks, partridges, and even swans. If fish was also served, they might have had eels, cod, bass, herring, and bluefish.

The Pilgrims may have eaten other birds besides turkey. However, the turkey is the bird that Americans usually eat on Thanksgiving Day.

Herring were just one of the many fish that Pilgrims may have eaten during the first Thanksgiving.

Other seafood at the feast might have been clams, mussels, and lobster.

Vegetables were also available to them. There were peas, beans, pumpkins, and other types of squash. There were also cranberries but no cranberry sauce.

Cakes, cookies, and pies were not served either. The Pilgrims had no flour left to bake with. So the Pilgrims might have made a boiled pumpkin pudding. They also had dried berries.

The feast lasted for three days. People mostly ate outdoors at long tables. There was not a building large enough to fit everyone inside.

However, there was more to this celebration than eating. The Wampanoags and Pilgrims also played games. They held

Cranberries were eaten raw by the Pilgrims.

36

footraces. The Pilgrims showed off their skill with **muskets**. They shot at targets. The Wampanoags did the same with bows and arrows.

The Pilgrims thought of the feast as a harvest celebration and a time for giving thanks. The Pilgrims were very religious. To them, giving thanks meant doing so in prayer. Along with eating and celebrating, the Pilgrims also gave thanks to God for the harvest.

Today we make pumpkin pie, but the Pilgrims used their pumpkins to make pudding.

As the years passed, the celebration took on a different meaning. People came to think of it as the first Thanksgiving. Yet that was not what it was for the Pilgrims and Wampanoag. It was just a time to feast and have fun.

THE PILGRIMS JUST ROASTED THEIR TURKEYS. THERE WAS NO STUFFING.

THIS TURKEY TASTES GOOD, BUT WHERE'S THE STUFFING?

37

10 Heading Home

In the years ahead, the Pilgrims faced many hardships. At times, the harvests did not provide enough food. Later on, there was trouble between the settlers and the Narragansett and Massachuset Indians. Yet, in time, more settlers arrived and the colony grew.

The Pilgrims made a lasting home for themselves in North America. These men and women would not be forgotten. They would come to be known as the European founders of New England. Students across the country still learn about them today.

Because of Samoset's brave entrance into the Plymouth colony, the Pilgrims quickly learned how to survive in America.

The Plymouth colony began to thrive after the first Thanksgiving. The Pilgrims soon were able to fill their homes with many useful items.

People still like the idea of the Pilgrim's thanksgiving feast. In 1941, Congress officially made Thanksgiving a federal holiday. For most Americans, it continues to be a wonderful day filled with family, friends, and feasting.

Max and I enjoyed our stay with the Pilgrims and the Wampanoag. But now we must be heading home. Max has some seeds that he wants to plant. He hopes to have his own harvest feast this year. We are glad you came along with us. Time travel is always more fun with friends. To the time machine!

Thanksgiving Day is a holiday celebrated by most Americans. Many big cities have parades to honor this very special day.

I DON'T THINK I'LL EVER BE ABLE TO VISIT NEW ENGLAND AGAIN WITHOUT THINKING ABOUT THE PILGRIMS.

YES, WITH THE WAMPANOAG'S HELP, THEY STARTED A NEW LIFE FOR THEMSELVES.

What Ever Happened To . . .

While time traveling, Max and I met some interesting people. We thought you might want to know what became of them.

WILLIAM BRADFORD

William Bradford served as the governor of Plymouth for over thirty years. Much of what we know about the colony comes from his writings. Bradford died in 1657.

MASSASOIT

This great Wampanoag chief signed a peace treaty with the Pilgrims and never broke the agreement. He remained a friend to the Pilgrims until his death in 1661.

SQUANTO

Though Squanto helped the Pilgrims, he also soon betrayed them. He told different American Indian groups that only he could stop the Pilgrims from attacking them. In return for doing so, these groups gave Squanto valuable gifts. But some of them also became very angry at the Pilgrims. Squanto died in 1622.

MILES STANDISH

Captain Miles Standish led the colony's small military force. He trained the men to defend themselves against the Narragansett and Massachuset Indians. Standish later helped start the Massachusetts town of Duxbury. He died in 1656.

Metacomet thought the Wampanoag's only chance for survival was to drive away the Pilgrims.

THE WAMPANOAG INDIANS

As the years passed, increasing numbers of Europeans arrived and settled on the Wampanoag's land. Massasoit's son, Metacomet, became leader of his people. He was called King Philip by the Europeans. He soon waged war on the Europeans for taking the Wampanoag's land. The two sides fought in what became known as King Philip's War. This fighting, as well as much disease, killed many Wampanoag. However, a small group of Wampanoag Indians still lives in the area. Some continue to celebrate their people's traditional festivals.

King Philip's War soon ended after Metacomet was killed.

Farewell Fellow Explorer,

I just wanted to take a moment to tell you about the real "Max and me." I am a children's book author and Max is a small, fluffy, white dog. I almost named him Marshmallow because of how he looked. However, he seems to think he's human—so only a more dignified name would do. Max also seems to think that he is a large, powerful dog. He fearlessly chases after much larger dogs in the neighborhood. Max was thrilled when the artist for this book drew him as a dog several times his size. He felt that someone in the art world had finally captured his true spirit.

In real life, Max is quite a traveler. I have taken him to nearly every state while doing research for different books. We live in Florida so when we go north I have to pack a sweater for him. When we were in Oregon it rained and I was glad I brought his raincoat. None of this gear is necessary when time traveling. My "take off" spot is the computer station and as always Max sits faithfully by my side.

Best Wishes,
Elaine & Max
(a small dog with big dreams)

43

Timeline

1620 September 6—The *Mayflower* sets sail for North America.

November 9—Land is spotted by those on the *Mayflower*.

November 11—The Mayflower Compact is completed and signed.

December 8—"The First Encounter" between the Pilgrims and the American Indians takes place.

December 11—The exploring party selects Plymouth as the site for their colony.

December 16—All the *Mayflower* passengers arrive at Plymouth.

1621 March 16—Samoset comes to Plymouth.

March 22—Samoset brings Squanto to meet the Pilgrims.

March 23—Massasoit signs peace treaty with Pilgrims.

March 31—Nearly half of the settlers at Plymouth have died.

April 5—The *Mayflower* sets sail for England.

Mid-October—The Pilgrims host a harvest celebration that later becomes known as the first Thanksgiving.

1622 December—Squanto becomes ill and dies while serving as a guide for the Pilgrims. At the time, they were exploring various parts of Cape Cod.

1941 The U.S. Congress officially makes Thanksgiving Day a federal holiday.

Words to Know

fertilizer—A substance applied to fields to make crops grow better.

maggots—The wormlike creatures that hatch from fly eggs.

moldy—Being covered with a furry fungus that grows on old food.

musket—An old-fashioned gun with a long barrel.

mussel—A type of shellfish.

palisade—A barrier built for protection.

pelt—An animal skin with the fur still on it.

savages—People who are thought to be uncivilized.

shallow—Not deep.

treaty—A formal agreement between two groups of people.

Further Reading

Bartlett, Robert Merrill. *The Story of Thanksgiving*. New York: HarperCollins, 2001.

DeKeyser, Stacy. *The Wampanoag*. Danbury, Conn.: Franklin Watts, 2005.

Erickson, Paul. *Daily Life In the Pilgrim Colony*. New York: Clarion Books, 2001.

Riehecky, Janet. *The Plymouth Colony*. Milwaukee: World Almanac Library, 2002.

Rosinsky, Natalie M. *The Wampanoag and Their History*. Minneapolis, Minn.: Compass Point Books, 2005.

Santella, Andrew. *The Plymouth Colony*. Minneapolis, Minn.: Compass Point Books, 2001.

Waters, Kate. *Giving Thanks: The 1621 Harvest Feast*. New York: Scholastic Press, 2001.

Whitehurst, Susan. *William Bradford and Plymouth: A Colony Grows*. New York: PowerKids Press, 2002.

Web Sites

The Mayflower Society

<http://www.mayflower.org>

This Web site is sponsored by the descendants of the Pilgrims who sailed on the Mayflower in 1620. There is a lot of interesting information on life in the new colony.

Pilgrim Hall Museum

<http://www.pilgrimhall.org>

Pilgrim Hall Museum's Web site has many interesting links about the Pilgrims' experience and Thanksgiving.

Plimoth Plantation

<http://www.plimoth.org>

Visit the Web site of a "living" museum that explores the history of Plymouth colony.

Do not miss the great photos here.

Index